RETHINK the MBA

**Why Business School is
Riskier Than You Think**

TABLE OF CONTENTS

INTRO
    My Story *1*
    Caveat Emptor *4*
    Offense and Defense *7*

WHAT'S AN MBA?
    It's Not an Investment *9*
    It's Not Unemployment Insurance *11*
    It's Not a Permanent Calling Card *14*
    It's a Gamble *17*

KNOW THE GAME
    Many Reasons to Get an MBA *19*
    Only One Good Reason *23*
    Only the Best Schools *25*

COUNT THE CHIPS
    Table Stakes *31*
    Our Strange American Ways *33*
    MBA Living Expenses *36*
    Levering Up *39*
    Opportunity Cost *41*
    Disappearing Paycheck *43*
    A Patek, a P85, and a Popo *46*
    Experience *49*
    Serendipity *52*

GOOD BETS
    Bankers *55*
    Consultants *58*

BREAK-EVEN BETS
    Career Switchers *61*
    Free Money *64*

SUCKER BETS
    College Grads *67*
    Learners *70*
    Part-timers *72*

Explorers *74*
Entrepreneurs *78*
Difference Makers *84*
Venture Capitalists *88*

MENTAL MISTAKES
Take the Easy Way *91*
Go to Learn *93*
Confuse Luck and Talent *95*
Ignore the Numbers *98*
Want A Break *100*
Believe Rationalizing Alumni *102*
Ignore the Counterfactual *104*

RETHINK THE MBA
Four Things *107*

To Evan

INTRO

My Story

I should never have gotten an MBA.

Eight years ago I decided to apply to business school in order to start my own company. For the entrepreneurs in the room this idea will sound hilarious (Hint: You don't need an MBA to start a company). Like all naïve dreams of glory, my dream was to find a co-founder, raise VC money after graduation, and wake up five years later partying with Elon Musk in Silicon Valley. I was planning to attend MIT until I was accepted off the wait list at Wharton. Since my wife was already getting her PhD at UPenn as well, I thanked my lucky stars and started there in the fall of 2007.

It was a fun two years. The majority of students and professors at Wharton were amazing, intelligent people, many of whom I still consider close friends. I was the Co-President of the Entrepreneurship Club and Co-Chair of the Entrepreneurship Conference, in case it wasn't already clear to you that I was really, really into being an "entrepreneur".

I graduated in 2009. I had no co-founder and no VC funding, but a stubborn commitment to push ahead anyway. I started a website to help people find contractors to make "green" home repairs. It was an interesting idea, but my own execution fell short, especially when it came time to pay the rent. It was now 2010, the economy was in the tank, and I needed to support my family. I started looking for work and doing consulting jobs on the side.

A year later, I finally found a job. Said another way, I was unemployed for a year after I shut down my company. At my new job, the starting salary was indeed higher than my pre-MBA job. Then, I started paying $1,300 a month in student loans and realized I had taken zero steps forward and two steps back.

I've spent a lot of time rethinking my decision to get an MBA. It took years for me to admit that I had made a mistake. The following essays started as a form of writing therapy. I decided to turn them into a book to help prospective MBA students. *I hope that's you.* I want to help you avoid the mistakes I made, and the mistakes I've seen others make in pursuit of an MBA.

You may think that an MBA is for everyone. It isn't. An MBA is for aspiring Bankers, Consultants, and maybe Fortune 100 middle managers. Everyone else is overpaying for the professional network, overpaying for the career advice, and overpaying to learn advanced business skills. Worst of all, a few people are completely wasting their time and money.

I should never have gone to business school. I'm

writing this book because there's a chance that maybe you shouldn't either.

It's time to rethink the MBA.

Caveat Emptor

This book is meant to be a conversation. I tried to write it to sound like I might sound over a cup of coffee. I'm not going to perform a detailed analysis of the pros and cons of getting an MBA. Instead, this book is the starting point for you to do your own analysis and draw your own conclusions about whether an MBA is right for you. Based on my experiences, I've developed some strong beliefs about the MBA. Let's get those on the table so you understand where I'm coming from.

I believe that the classes, alumni network, and career options of an MBA all have value. However, they're not always as valuable as their cost in time and tuition. I believe only a few career paths are really worth the cost required to get an MBA: Banking and Consulting. Other career paths, like middle management in the Fortune 100, are harder to justify. A few career paths, like entrepreneurship or non-profit work, are simply not worth it.

I believe that the decision to get an MBA, regardless of career path, has more risk than you think. There's the risk of spending too much money on trips and events of questionable value. There's the risk of wasting too much time exploring a huge number of career paths. There's the risk of getting sucked into career paths you didn't go to b-school to pursue in the first place. I don't believe most prospective MBA students really understand these risks.

I believe that you have to frame big choices in life using language that enables you to make the best decision. Throughout this book, I frame the MBA decision in the language of gambling. I'm not saying b-schools are equivalent to casinos, where the house always wins and the student players always lose. I'm just saying that like gambling, there are both winners *and* losers in b-school. If I can convince you that pursuing an MBA is like gambling, then hopefully you'll be more careful about spending your time and money to get one.

I believe you should read this book to *avoid* being a loser at the MBA game. I hope this book will help you think about the things you *should not do* before applying to b-school. I hope you'll be inspired to think about every possible way to achieve your career goals, in addition to attending business school. If you take the time to rethink the MBA, I believe you'll end up feeling more confident about your decision to either get one or not.

I believe b-schools need to reform the MBA so that the odds of winning are much higher for students. For starters, b-schools should get rid of the two-year MBA. One year is enough. INSEAD, a top-ranked b-school in France, is only one-year long and their graduates seem to do just fine. B-schools should also stop recruiting aspiring entrepreneurs. Aspiring entrepreneurs don't need two years of training. They need to "fail fast" through the process of actually trying to start a business. Instead, b-schools should offer startup accelerator programs, or nothing at all.

I believe financial planning and career counseling services should be provided for all accepted students. None of these services are offered to students today, and so too many students get an MBA for the wrong reasons, and pay a huge amount of money in the process. Prospectives need to be nudged to think about their finances and their goals. They also need to be given the option to cancel their enrollment if they discover any of these things aren't aligned with the cost and time of an MBA.

I believe b-schools should do everything possible to make sure getting an MBA is a winnable bet for every student.

I believe every student should be a winner if they spend the time and money to get an MBA.

Offense and Defense

I'm not alone in choosing an MBA for the wrong reasons. Every year, a third of prospective students think their MBA will lead to an entrepreneurial career.[i] Far less actually pursue entrepreneurship after graduation. This means they either changed their mind, or were diverted from their original goals. Even the students that persevere and start a company are burdened with two years of tuition and time, on top of the costs of starting a company.

Similarly, nearly two thirds of prospectives want to improve their leadership skills.[ii] But, through volunteering or dedicated training, these skills could be honed for a lot less money than an MBA. Many people also get an MBA to develop business skills or explore careers. However, there are many free alternatives that accomplish the same things.

Fewer people should get an MBA, and those that do should go for the right reasons.

I may not be alone, but I'm also not a victim looking for something to blame. I made my own mistakes. Believe me, I'm still paying for them. I'm also not suggesting that Wharton, my mentors, or my friends were responsible for my decision to get an MBA. I was. This isn't a victim story, but I'll tell you what it is…

I read stories every day of people that succeed despite the odds…the rich and famous survivors.

But, I don't think these success stories are valuable, except for entertainment. Many people did similar things and failed. It's called survivorship bias. Instead, the most useful stories come from failures. You learn what *not* to do. This book isn't a victim story, it's *a failure story*. It's based on the many ways I failed to think through my decision to get an MBA. That's what makes it valuable. That's why you should read it.

I'm not trying to degrade anyone with an MBA. I have an MBA and so do many of my closest friends. The critical things I have to say about the MBA degree are not criticisms of people who have MBAs, or people who work in business schools. My only intention is to help people to learn from my mistakes.

Finally, I appreciate irony. I realize that I can write this book because I have a top tier MBA. However, I didn't go to Wharton to earn the credibility to write a book! Who the hell wants to write a book about overpaying for an entrepreneurial education? I would much rather be doing something else in my spare time. But, these are the cards I've got, so I'm playing them.

WHAT'S AN MBA?

It's Not an Investment

I hate the phrase "an MBA is an investment". It may be linguistically accurate, since it's possible to estimate the costs and benefits of getting an MBA. The problem is that the casual way this phrase is used has many unspoken implications that aren't true.

The first unspoken implication is that the cost of an MBA doesn't matter because you're guaranteed to make your money back over time. In other words, even if an MBA has a low rate of return, it's still greater than zero. Unfortunately, I'm living proof that it's possible to pay for an MBA and have a negative rate of return. If you use the term "investment" loosely, you risk missing this point.

The second unspoken implication of the word "investment" is the idea that an MBA has significant durable value, like say, a house. The thinking is that just like you can always live in a house, you'll always have the MBA knowledge in your brain. Therefore, the value of an MBA would seem to be as permanent as a house. But, it isn't. The knowledge goes away if you don't use it. Furthermore, the MBA has the highest amount of value when applying to your first job out of b-school, and much less value for each subsequent job. Finally, who knows if an MBA will be worth anything in the future? Just because it was a safe bet last century, doesn't mean it will be a safe bet in this one.

The final unspoken implication is that if you don't "invest" in an MBA, you're not making an investment at all. In other words, instead of "investing in yourself", you're doing something else. Of course, you can "invest in yourself" and your education without spending any money. Reading a book, taking a free class online, or learning by doing are all "investments" in knowledge. We just don't call them "investments" because they don't cost anything!

For these reasons, you'd be right to call an MBA an "investment", but it's better to call it something else. You don't want to accidentally assume an MBA always has a positive ROI, is infinitely durable, or is the only investment you can make in your career growth. It doesn't, it isn't, and there are many other investments you can make in your career that would be just as valuable.

It's Not Unemployment Insurance

Before b-school, I thought an MBA was "unemployment insurance". In other words, if I had a top tier MBA, I would always have a job and a paycheck. In b-school this assumptions was also widespread. The cost of an MBA was viewed as a "deductible" for never having to worry about finding a job again.

Of course the truth is that MBA grads become unemployed just like everyone else. It may be less likely than if you only have a bachelors degree, but it can still happen. Economic cycles come and go. Employers make lay offs. You will struggle to find work sometimes. You will sometimes just have to dust yourself off, pick yourself up, and get out there and hustle. Of course, you'll be hustling for a job at a consulting firm while the guy with a GED is hustling for a job at Wal-Mart. But either way, you'll be unemployed.

This isn't just me, and this isn't just our modern economy. After I shut down my startup to look for work, I met many people with top tier MBAs, from every age group, and every professional level, who simply couldn't find a job. This wasn't a case of "being picky" waiting for the "perfect job". This was twelve to eighteen months of people pounding the pavement and looking in many different career areas to find something. We all called ourselves "consultants", but we were all unemployed.

The most important thing for you to understand is that the career opportunities for MBA graduates are very unevenly distributed. While you're pursuing your MBA, you're recruiting for mid-level jobs with companies from every industry specifically looking to hire newly minted MBAs. Relevant experience is nice to have, but not required.

After graduation, you're no longer an MBA student; you're an "experienced candidate". Now an MBA is one of a lengthy list of pre-qualifications for a job, as opposed to the primary one. Worse, the number of job opportunities for MBA graduates is limited to the industry you chose after b-school.

This explains the unemployment phenomenon for MBA grads, even from top tier schools. In b-school, it's all about your potential ability. Afterwards, it's all about your experience. If you're "experienced" in an industry that gets hit hard by the economy, you're going to be hit hard as well. You can try and switch industries, but you'll no longer have any significant advantages versus a fresh MBA grad. And, why would an employer want to hire an old dog when they can just teach the young dog new tricks?

They wouldn't.

So, don't believe the unemployment myth. It will cause you to be overly confident about your decision to get an MBA, because you can rationalize away all the downside to your decision. Rationalize all you want, but I'm here to tell you that the downside exists, whether you believe it or not.

It's Not a Permanent Calling Card

There's an adage that "where you go to college only matters for your first job". The implication is that afterwards, what you do in your first job is more important than where you went to school. For example, if you spend two years at Goldman Sachs after undergrad (from State U) and so does someone else (from Harvard), you're both effectively "the same" two years after college.

I believe this adage is approximately true for b-school. Having the brand of a top b-school on your resume will *not* transform your reputation into a bulletproof calling card for the rest of your life. If you spend two years as a Product Manager at Google (with an MBA) and another guy does too (no MBA, just a programmer), you both look like Product Managers from Google to the next firm that hires you.

For example, it has been five years since I graduated from b-school. It would be ridiculous for me to start a conversation with a potential employer with a line about my Wharton MBA. Instead, I would explain what I'm doing now and what I've done recently in my current job. In fact, if I were to bring up my MBA in the beginning of a conversation, they might assume that what I'm doing now just isn't that interesting or important.

There's another element of the MBA calling card you may be tempted to significantly overvalue: the alumni network. Of course, you can always name drop your alma mater to get a conversation started, but then what? Like any other conversation with a stranger, if you don't have something compelling to say, the conversation isn't going to go anywhere. The other problem is that you could probably find a hundred other ways to get a conversation started with someone important. You don't have to spend $200,000 to have something in common to talk about.

If you want a permanent calling card, permanently do interesting things! Whatever you're doing right now will be the most interesting thing about you. Where you got your MBA is only interesting to the company interviewing you during your second year at b-school. After that, it's just old news.

—

One caveat: I don't want to dismiss the importance of the first job after graduation and the value of the alumni network to get it. An MBA is never a more valuable calling card than when you're in b-school. You can freely harass alumni as an unemployed, job-seeking "student". (If you're unemployed and job seeking at any other point in your career, these e-mails and intros will be much less welcome). Similarly, the sheer number of job opportunities will never be higher in b-school compared to any other point in your career. You have to exploit these two facts to the maximum.

My ultimate point is this: You are probably

significantly *overestimating* the relevance of a name brand MBA five years after graduation and completely *underestimating* its relevance before graduation. During b-school, the name brand is all that matters. It dictates which employers are there to recruit you. After your first job, where you went to school won't be more than a conversation starter and you'll only get "recruited" for what you've done since graduation.

It's A Gamble

An MBA is not literally a "gamble", but I'm going to call it that anyway. I know that gambling involves playing games with a random outcome. I also know that you don't get a job at Goldman Sachs by spinning a roulette wheel. But, even if you don't play roulette, there are several reasons why calling an MBA a "gamble" makes sense. Simply put, framing the MBA choice as a "gamble" enables you to make the best decision.

Just as in gambling, there are "table stakes" to play the MBA game. But, forget a $20 blind in poker. In order to walk into the b-school "casino" you'll pay an average of $200,000. Imagine that you were going to play a game of poker that lasted for two years and cost $200,000 to play! You would probably spend months doing nothing but studying the game of poker. Unfortunately, you can easily spend months just getting into the b-school casino, and spend barely any time studying how to play the two-year MBA game. If you think of the MBA as a gamble, it will help you realize that the game is just as important as where you play.

After you've put up your table stakes, you have to choose your bets. You can put all your chips on one career path, or several. You can bet on career paths where the odds are against you (Entrepreneurship) or where the odds are in your favor (Consulting). You can even just place a lot of different bets once you get to the table. Your decisions will have a big impact on your likelihood of "winning".

Bets are risky. It's good to feel this sense of risk when you're playing the MBA game. Why? Even the "good bets" like Consulting don't always pay out. Not everyone gets to work at McKinsey, BCG, and Bain. If you can't work for one of these guys, is the MBA bet worth it to you? This is more than just bragging rights. Even at top schools, the salary range for "good bets" like Consulting is still significant. Someone has to accept an offer from a low ranked consulting firm and make $90,000 a year with no signing bonus. That someone could be you.

Finally, gambling doesn't feel like a smart thing to do with your money. Usually, you only gamble with money that you aren't afraid to completely lose. Well, if you don't do everything possible to win the MBA game, you risk losing a lot of time and money. If that would be devastating for you, you shouldn't play.

If you've never thought of an MBA in these terms, now's the time to start. Take your decision very seriously. I believe you'll make the best decision possible when you feel the risk in your gut and stop thinking of an MBA as an investment, unemployment insurance, or a permanent calling card. Treat the MBA like a gamble, and then play accordingly.

KNOW THE GAME

Many Reasons to Get an MBA

Many people want to attend b-school for reasons that sound credible and convincing aside from specific career ambitions. That's because at face value these reasons would in fact be personally and professionally valuable. The problem is that these reasons are always presented in isolation from the costs of b-school. They seem great, but their cost-adjusted value is debatable.

I have a simple heuristic to separate the good and bad reasons to get an MBA. Remember the game you play at a Chinese restaurant where you add the phrase "in bed" to the end of every fortune in a fortune cookie? To play the b-school version, you add the phrase "for $200,000" to the end of the common reasons to get an MBA. It quickly puts the value of these "reasons" in perspective. Let's play a few rounds using "reasons" that you might find on certain famous b-school websites.

Get a "global" mindset (for $200,000):

Many b-schools highlight their student diversity as an opportunity to expand your mind about different points of view. If you currently work on a farm in South Dakota, this reason might be worth the money. Personally, before b-school I lived in a racially and culturally diverse neighborhood in Philadelphia and worked for a Spanish company. Did b-school radically change my thinking, mindset, or group of friends relative to these other experiences? No.

I'm guessing that you probably don't work on a farm in South Dakota. Instead, you've worked, lived, and travelled to places that have already expanded your way of thinking to a global level. You probably even maintain your global perspective with a $200 subscription to The Economist magazine. Well, you can read The Economist for 1,000 years for $200,000.

Become a "leader" (for $200,000):

The idea that you will become a "leader" with an MBA is misleading. Worse, it conveys the inverse message that you can't be a leader without one! It's so vague and general that you can say it about almost anything. If a business school marketer worked for a scuba diving company, you would read about how "breathing underwater reinforces a sense of calm that will help you become a better leader". Does this mean you should pay $50,000 to live in Australia for six months to become a Divemaster on the Great Barrier Reef? No. You learn leadership by trying to lead in whatever you do or in whatever interests you. Pick a problem that needs to be solved and ask other people to help you solve it. You are now "leading". No scuba diving equipment or MBA required.

Learn by doing (for $200,000):

There seems to be some confusion in business school about what "doing" actually means. It's extremely difficult to "do" anything in b-school aside from attend classes, study, and perform countless team-based learning assignments. Most of the "hands on" class projects, even at their best, are poor proxies for the "real world" that the word "doing" is supposed to imply. The only true "learning by doing" experiences in b-school are the following: organizing clubs and conferences, interviewing, and drinking beer. Everything else is "learning by learning".

Access an amazing alumni network (for $200,000):

Yes, it's amazing! You can randomly e-mail another alumni and say you're also an alumni from the same school. During school, this may help you get a job. After graduation, this strategy is usually as successful as e-mailing any other complete stranger. Consider this: After five years, I have *classmates* that won't even respond to my e-mails, let alone alumni who graduated in a different year. More to the point, in the Digital Age you can find and connect with anyone on LinkedIn, Twitter, or Facebook. For any person you want to connect with, you can find some alternative, completely free, way. And if you don't have an MBA from their school, so what? Find some other connection you have with them and make it happen.

Hopefully, you'll find my heuristic useful for separating the good reasons from the bad ones. In general, I find that most of the non-career reasons to attend b-school are just meant to stroke your ego, regardless of whether they make any economic sense. These "reasons" tend to be variations of the same theme: you will become a "leader" and a member of a "unique" group of people… *if you have an MBA.*

The phony reasons to get an MBA remind me of the ads for Patek Philippe watches. These ads never mention the expensive materials or complicated engineering. There's just a picture of some guy who is clearly an amazing, successful dad, leaving his legacy (symbolized by his watch) to his perfect little children. Who wouldn't want to be that guy?! Fuck, I desperately want to be that guy! Fortunately, you can't take out a student loan to buy a $25,000 watch. If you could, I would have a couple of these watches already ("But honey…I'll hand it down the to next generation!"). Obviously, you don't suddenly become some incredible super-dad by owning a fancy Swiss watch.

Well, you don't become an amazing, globetrotting, entrepreneurial leader just because you have an MBA.

Only One Good Reason

There's only one good reason to get an MBA: to get your Dream Job. Your Dream Job should be nearly impossible to get without one. If you want an MBA for any other reason, please rethink your decision. You're about to spend $200,000 and leave the workforce for two years. If you can't get your Dream Job after spending all that time and money, why the hell would you get an MBA? To answer this question, let's flip it on its head: why *shouldn't* you get an MBA?

You shouldn't get an MBA if you can't get your Dream Job after b-school without making substantial financial sacrifices to pay for it. For example, if you have to finance your MBA and your Dream Job involves working to alleviate poverty in India, there's no place that will pay you enough to afford a modest lifestyle *and* your student loans. Being an entrepreneur, or working for startups, non-profits, political organizations, or schools, are all great examples of Dream Jobs that may just be dreams after you graduate with an MBA.

You also shouldn't get an MBA if you could get your Dream Job in a more direct and cost-effective way. If you could get a good job today and work your way up to a Dream Job tomorrow, then you shouldn't get an MBA. If you can take an unpaid internship, move to a different city, or hire a headhunter to find your Dream Job, then you should seriously consider all of these options before getting an MBA.

Ultimately, the MBA decision boils down to two things: finance and focus. If your Dream Job won't pay you enough to afford an MBA, don't get one. If taking two years to sit in a classroom is a detour from getting your Dream Job, you should find a more direct path. In order to examine both of these issues rationally, you need to check your Swiss Banker ego at the door. People at cocktail parties will think it's pretty cool that you have an MBA from Harvard Business School. However, if you don't have your Dream Job, it won't matter. You'll be unhappy.

Focus on your dreams. Forget about the cocktail parties.

Only the Best Schools

You would think that *business* school is all about learning *business skills*. It's not. That's just the official excuse to spend two years not working. B-school is actually just a means for providing highly vetted job applicants to the human resource departments of large employers. Employers can't afford to run background checks and grade application essays for every single applicant. But, you're happy to pay for all of this when you apply to b-school! This makes an employer's job very easy when it comes to hiring. Now, employers can simply judge you according to the rank of b-school you attend, along with a few interviews to confirm that you know what you're doing and are a good fit for their company.

Employers don't judge you primarily by the business skills you learn in b-school. If they did, you could get a job at Goldman Sachs by getting straight A's in a part-time MBA program at "State U" just as easily as you could by getting straight A's at HBS. You can't. It's not because HBS has better professors, higher quality course content, or nicer classrooms, and therefore their students are more "skilled" (even assuming all those things are true). It's because the abilities of the students at State U are not as high as those at HBS *on average.* If you were Goldman Sachs, would you recruit where the *average* student had a 95% GMAT score or a 50% GMAT score? Exactly. That's what b-school is all about.

You can prove this to yourself by imagining that HBS could *only* accept students who were in the lowest 10% of GMAT performers each year and "State U" could *only* accept students from the top 10% of GMAT performers. Over time, the amazing professors and fancy classrooms at HBS wouldn't matter. Their graduates would be less impressive businesspeople, and their reputation with employers would eventually suffer. On the other hand, "State U" would eventually be crawling with recruiters from McKinsey and Goldman Sachs after they figured out that it was the new HBS.

Hopefully now it's obvious why getting into the "best" b-school matters so much. You're going to the "best" school so that you can be with the "best" students and attract the "best" employers.

There's an incredible irony to this entire process. The primary value of b-school is the market signal of your abilities. This is derived from the rank of the b-school that decides to accept your application. The application process determines your abilities using proxies that you already possessed before attending b-school (e.g. your GPA and GMAT scores). The cost of the application process is trivial…perhaps a few hundred dollars for some students and administrators to review and approve your application. In contrast, the primary cost of b-school stems from professor's salaries and expensive classrooms. In other words, the primary cost and the primary value of an MBA are not closely related.

To review: The application and branding process costs b-schools virtually nothing, but is incredibly valuable for you. On the other hand, you could learn the business skills on your own for virtually nothing, but you will pay $200,000 for tenured professors to explain these skills to you in a very nice classroom.

It gets worse.

When it comes to the proxies for ability, such as GMAT scores or GPA, there are many more qualified applicants than open spaces at the best schools. The best schools get to choose amazing students from an applicant pool of incredible students. This means that there are many students who are as good as the "best" but won't be perceived as the "best" by the market. Why? Because there weren't enough classrooms and chairs to allow these students to attend the best schools.

This means there are hundreds, or even thousands, of people who could have gone to HBS or Stanford or Wharton in a luckier universe. On the other hand, since they didn't have their previously acquired abilities validated after the fact by a famous university, employers will treat them differently, and they will likely perceive their own self-worth differently as well.

The admissions process is capricious and unfair to say the least. If you learn the skills and have the abilities, you should have a chance to compete against everyone else at your level.

You might not because there are only a few hundred chairs in the classrooms at the "best" b-schools.

—

There are a few solutions to the problems above.

Business schools could establish transparent standards for admission, and in the event they have too few seats to handle the demand, simply choose students by lottery. Of course, there will still be a lot of people that don't get to go to HBS. However, in this world those same students could prove they were good enough to go. Then, they could confidently pursue their business skills training at another b-school knowing that they wouldn't be discriminated against by employers.

Educational entrepreneurs could provide a 3rd party certification system for b-school students to allow them to claim they were "good enough" for the Top 3 (or Top 10) b-schools. The certification could be based on GMAT scores alone, or on more extensive application materials. Either way, it would enable students to demonstrate their capabilities without having to pay for the MBA. Imagine if this educational startup was successful enough to convince employers that students with their certification were as good as graduates of the best schools? Talk about competition: a $100 certification vs. a $200,000 MBA.

Finally, smart employers should understand that

b-schools are unnecessarily inflating the costs of their workforce. A top MBA brand is mostly just providing information about a student that an employer could have found out three years earlier by asking applicants for GMAT scores, GPAs, and application essays. If I were Google, I would openly advertise nice signing bonuses to people who handed in their HBS or Stanford acceptance letters for a "Product Manager in Training" job. I'd take 50% of the expected salary I'd have to pay them if they had their MBA, and use it for signing bonuses and targeted training. Google would pay less cash overall, and students would get the awesome job they wanted without the cost and two-year professional detour.

In the meantime, until any one of these things happens, you'll just have to accept the rules if you decide to play the MBA game.

COUNT THE CHIPS

Table Stakes

In poker, you need to put cash on the table just to play the game. It's called "table stakes". In b-school, the table stakes are two years of time and $200,000 before you can bet on your future career path. If you go to most b-school websites you can easily find the cost of tuition and living expenses. It's much harder to figure out the additional hidden expenses like partying and traveling, or the cost of student loans to pay for it all. And you're certainly not going to find any discussion of the intangible costs. You'll have to keep reading for that.

One of the biggest mistakes I made was never fully calculating the table stakes of an MBA until the first time I signed my student loan documents. Obviously, by then it was a little late to reconsider whether or not I wanted to put so many chips on the table! I don't think I'm alone. Many people think the cost of an MBA doesn't require much due diligence. This goes back to the "investment" framing problem I mentioned earlier. This framing fools you into thinking that the MBA "investment" is so good that you don't need to add up the table stakes before you play.

In my case, most of my mentors told me I would be an idiot not to go to Wharton if I had the chance. All of them, including myself, had the unquestioned assumption that a top tier MBA pays for itself over time. Of course, this assumption is highly dependent on having a Dream Job that requires an MBA. In fairness to my mentors, I don't think they knew this. Of course, I didn't either.

Despite what you or your mentors may think, you're *not* an idiot to take some time to reflect on the massive pile of money it takes to get an MBA. Walk around the block and think about taking out $200,000 in student loans at 7% fixed interest that you'll be paying off for 10-25 years after graduation. The single most important thing you can do before you decide to get an MBA is to add up the table stakes based on your personal situation. It takes a lot of money to play the MBA game. Figure out how much money you need long before you start your first semester.

Our Strange American Ways

The average cost of a two-year MBA from a Top-10 school in the U.S. is $200,000 in tuition and living expenses.[iii] An obvious question is: Why is this number so high? The easy answer is that great professors and nice classrooms are expensive. That's true, but what about the fact that in the U.S. an MBA takes two years to get instead of one? It sounds like a stupid question, but INSEAD, one of the best b-schools in the world, has a one-year program and their graduates do just fine in the job market. Why?

It could be that the professors at INSEAD are twice as good as the professors at HBS, Wharton and Stanford. However, I had a few INSEAD professors at Wharton and they were exactly the same quality as the Wharton professors. Or, it could be that INSEAD graduates are half as good as their peers with a two-year MBA, but employers just haven't figured it out yet. I really doubt it. INSEAD graduates get jobs at large, multi-national companies that seek out the best talent globally and could easily compare graduate quality between INSEAD and other top schools.

The only real difference is that in the U.S. we have the dubious privilege of getting to major in a subject like Finance or Marketing in our second year of b-school. Unfortunately, this major doesn't seem to have any real impact on the salaries of U.S. MBA graduates. If it did, U.S. MBAs would get paid a lot more than their

INSEAD counterparts. They don't. There are of course minor pay differences between INSEAD and other top schools, but these are due to differences in brand value, not time spent sitting in class.

My conclusion: Two-year MBA students are paying for one year they don't need.

Why are students in the U.S. still burdened by the two-year MBA? It's probably a historic relic from when the MBA was first dreamed up as a degree. Now it's done this way because that's how it's always been done. After all, who's going to change things? Employers don't pay for MBAs (usually), so they aren't incentivized to push for a shorter degree. If they switched to one-year MBAs, b-schools would be forced to churn out more students in order to stay revenue neutral. This would risk diluting their brand and increasing their operating costs, which means they're not incentivized either. Ultimately, students pay for the extra year because no one else in incentivized to care.

—

The situation above is bad for students, but on the plus side it has an extremely simple solution: American b-schools should get rid of the second year of b-school. They could even improve on INSEAD's model by offering a one-year "general" MBA or a one-year "major" MBA. The "general" MBA would be like the MBA core classes today. The "major" MBA would be composed of a mix of MBA core classes and higher-level courses in a specific subject. Students could take the "major" MBA by testing out of core classes before enrollment. For example, if you were in Banking prior to b-school and could test out of basic accounting and finance, you could free up class time to pursue a major in Marketing. These "major" MBAs would still be a year long, but allow students with significant business backgrounds to specialize, instead of relearning what they already know.

This solution would be easy to implement. At Wharton, for example, there is already a test out mechanism for core courses. However, even if you test out of a semester's worth of classes, you're still stuck taking other classes for two years to get your MBA. Wharton could just as easily allow students to graduate early if they tested out of core classes. If Wharton could do it, so could every other business school.

Every business school should.

Unfortunately, this solution is not likely to happen because it's not in the interests of b-schools to have you pay less tuition. So, understand that if you're going anywhere but INSEAD, you're going to pay for a year of classes that isn't going to add much career value, just make the MBA table stakes twice as high.

MBA Living Expenses

To calculate how much an MBA is really going to cost you, the starting point is to add up the tuition and living expenses at the b-school you'd like to attend. Since I have no idea which one that is, here's the math for the Top-10 U.S. MBA programs and INSEAD as of 2012 as a conversation starter.[iv] I'm including INSEAD to emphasize how expensive our two-year American MBA tradition really is.

THE COST OF AN MBA			
	Program Cost	Living Expenses	Total
University of Chicago	$116,969	$89,274	$206,243
Harvard University	$133,961	$91,200	$225,161
University of Pennsylvania	$127,176	$94,835	$222,011
Stanford University	$122,400	$93,866	$216,266
Duke University	$114,842	$78,083	$192,925
Cornell University	$111,896	$78,128	$190,024
University of Michigan	$104,789	$71,426	$176,215
MIT	$122,880	$92,827	$215,707
University of Virginia	$99,800	$74,724	$174,524
Average	$117,190	$84,929	$202,120
INSEAD	$71,718	$30,344	$102,062

These are very big numbers you've probably seen before. However, we're not done. We also have to add a few more numbers you've probably never heard of called "MBA Living Expenses".

You've never heard of MBA Living Expenses because you've never been to b-school. In addition to the things you actually need like food and rent (the "Living Expenses" above), most MBA students also spend tons of money in bars and restaurants with their MBA buddies on nights and weekends. They also spend tons of money going to the MBA Poker Tournament in Las Vegas. Then, they spend tons more traveling to the Patagonia for an MBA "Leadership" Trek. A few of the really crazy ones spend tons and tons and tons of money ($15,000 to $20,000 or nearly 10% of the cost of an MBA) for a trip to Antarctica. These costs are not on any b-school website, but you'll pay for them when you arrive and see all your friends doing these "once in a lifetime opportunities" as well.

I guesstimate that MBA Living Expenses are a cool $28,400 in total: about $800 per month for dinners and drinks on the town, $5,000 per year for two international trips, and $2,000 per year spent on four domestic trips, like long weekends.[v] In total, plus or minus a few trips to Vegas or the Patagonia, you're looking down the barrel of $230,000 for a two-year MBA. B-schools should provide more data to students about the average cost of the trips, clubs, and social activities. MBA Living Expenses can add up quickly.

Thankfully, I was able to pay less than $230,000 for my MBA, but not easily. Unlike many of my peers, I rarely went out to eat at restaurants, never went to look at penguins in Antarctica, and lived in a modest neighborhood in Philly. I'd saved some money by my late 20's, but I had also gotten married, bought an engagement ring, went on a honeymoon, and bought a car. I wasn't exactly rolling in almost a quarter million bucks in cash. So, like any good American, I borrowed the rest. This is where the table stakes get really high.

Levering Up

Leverage is the hidden cost of b-school. Students take on different amounts of debt, so few b-schools feel the need to estimate its cost and put it on their websites. Most students only figure out the cost of leverage once they've started school. Even worse, despite the fact that interest rates are at historic lows, most student loans are backed by the Federal Government and have much higher fixed interest rates.

If you calculate the present value of all your interest payments over a 10, 15, or 20 year period, you get the numbers below.[vi] This assumes that you have to finance 100% of your $230,000 in MBA costs: tuition, living expenses, and MBA Living Expenses. I know this is the worst-case scenario, but it will give you a feel for how much more expensive an MBA can be after you lever up.[vii]

INTEREST PAYMENTS ON STUDENT DEBT	
Term of Loans	Total Payments
10 Years	$55,993
15 Years	$79,125
20 Years	$98,058

If you have to use debt to pay for an MBA, the total cost is somewhere between $260,000 and $300,000 in total out of pocket costs. In other words, when you add debt, you're paying for the equivalent of an extra semester to an extra year of b-school.

The implications of leverage are obvious to me,

because three times each month Citibank extracts a pound of flesh from my bank account. However, let me bring these numbers home to you with a "fun" example. I was talking to a fellow Wharton alum who is a Partner at a Venture Capital fund and probably ten years older than me. The conversation somehow went from sports to family to me complaining about my student loans. The "fun" surprise was that *he* then started complaining about *his* student loans as well. I couldn't believe it.

I know there are jobs out there with bonus structures that could take down the numbers above in a couple of years, especially if you're single or don't have kids. I'm sure some of my former classmates in Consulting or Banking are already debt free. I also know that these numbers will be different based on your specific circumstances: personal savings, scholarships, interest rates, etc. The point is that no matter what your circumstances or career path look like, the numbers above should really make you scared. It's safe to say that for anyone who isn't a millionaire, $200,000 to $300,000 is a huge amount of money to bet on a new career path.

It had better be worth it.

Opportunity Cost

As if tuition, living expenses, MBA Living Expenses, and financing costs were not enough, we still need to talk about "opportunity cost". This is the geeky economics term for the two years of earnings you miss by deciding to get an MBA. To calculate this number, you can't just add up two years of your former salary. The IRS would have taken a piece and much of the rest would've gone towards the living expenses we already took into consideration.

The easiest way to calculate opportunity cost is to figure out how much of your post-tax dollars you're able to save each year when you're working full-time. Today you might put away some cash into a savings account, stocks, or your 401k. When you're getting an MBA, you're not putting away anything. When you're a student, you don't borrow money to save it, you only borrow what you need for living expenses, tuition, and traveling to Antarctica. So if you figure out how much money you're currently able to save before starting school, and multiply it by two, that's roughly your opportunity cost to get an MBA.

I'm telling you now to add the opportunity cost to the MBA table stakes, but most people don't. No one who goes to b-school really wants to stay in his or her current job, so they don't think about the lost money associated with it. Instead, they focus on how much money they'll be making in two years. In other words, it's hard to want the lost dollars because they would have come at the expense of getting a completely new, post-MBA job.

Opportunity cost dollars also never touch your hands, so you don't really feel like you ever lost them. However, you'll probably feel it when you graduate. It's another two years of savings you would've had for a down payment on a house or a new car. For this reason, it deserves to be added to the giant pile of table stakes we've already calculated. I can't put an exact number on it because it will vary from person to person. For me, it was about $40,000 in total.

Honestly, I'd rather not think about it.

Disappearing Paycheck

An MBA is a bet you place to find your Dream Job. You bet a huge pile of money. Hopefully you win, but it's possible to lose. But let's forget about winning or losing for a second and just talk about breaking even. I've said that tuition, living expenses, and MBA Living Expenses add up to about $230,000. If you take the worst-case scenario and finance everything, let's figure out the annual pay increase you'll need to make in your post-MBA job just to pay your annual student loans and break-even.[viii]

BREAK-EVEN SALARY INCREASE NEEDED TO PAY FOR AN MBA			
Term of Loan	Monthly Post-tax Loans	Monthly Pre-tax Cost	Annual Salary Increase to Break-Even
10 Years	$2,710	$4,169	$50,028
15 Years	$2,083	$3,204	$38,448
20 Years	$1,785	$2,746	$32,958

As you can see, you're going to need to make $30,000 to $50,000 per year in additional salary just to break-even after you graduate. This is why you have to really understand whether your Dream Job can pay you enough money to make the MBA worthwhile. Before you perform this analysis, be sure to adjust the numbers above for your specific circumstances. You have to adjust for any savings or scholarship money you're able to bring to the table and for the exact interest rates and tuition you're going to have.

On the other hand, you may also have to make adjustments that will make the numbers even higher. We've assumed that your life will stay the same after graduation. However, you're probably going to move to a new city, or get married, or even have kids. All of these things will potentially add a lot more money to the break-even requirements.

For example, I went to business school in Philadelphia, then moved to Boston, then had a baby one year after graduating. My rent more than doubled after moving to Boston, and then I added childcare costs a year later. I then moved to the San Francisco Bay Area, which makes the rents in Boston seem downright rational. Despite these life changes, I still have to eat food, heat my apartment, and wear clothes to work, let alone pay for student loans. I've had to make a lot of compromises and they're not fun. For the first year after I started paying childcare expenses, I stopped making my 401k contributions. It was an easy choice. I could: save for retirement, pay for childcare, or pay my student loans. Retirement lost.

Hopefully I've made myself clear. The cost of an MBA is *fucking insane*.

—

B-schools could do far more to help students calculate the table stakes of an MBA, long before they're signing the loan documents for their first semester. Simply listing the aggregate cost numbers on a website is not enough. Students need tools to help them estimate the true costs of attendance based on their exact levels of debt and tuition. Better tools are also needed to figure out the career paths that would enable a student to break-even. Case studies of actual students would be invaluable.

Furthermore, every student should be required to complete an online financial model for his or her financial situation before enrollment. Most importantly, there should be a "satisfaction guarantee". In other words, students should have the option *not to enroll* if it turns out that their career path doesn't make economic sense. If b-schools are truly adding value to a student's career, the extra financial insight will simply confirm the value of the time and tuition. If there's no value-add, students should know and b-schools have a duty to help them figure this out.

Until b-schools make these changes, however, you need to get yourself out of the "b-school is an investment" mindset like I was. If you don't know your break-even salary post-MBA, you have some financial modeling to do. It's your responsibility to know exactly what it would mean to "win" at b-school. Do it before you receive an acceptance letter. It's literally the most important thing you can do to ensure that you are making the MBA decision with your eyes wide open.

A Patek, a P85, and a Popo

It can be hard to wrap your mind around big numbers. So, let's just have a little fun and visualize the amount of money we're talking about for an MBA. Here are just a handful of the crazy, fun things you could buy that cost as much or less than what an MBA might cost you.

For **$25,000** you can buy a Patek Philippe Calatrava, the watch I will be handing down to the "next generation" in my next life as a Swiss banker.[ix] Patek Philippe is one of the few watch companies left in the world making their own automatic movements. Their watches are beautiful, timeless, and the cost of your first quarter of b-school.

For **$50,000** you can dine at the French Laundry, arguably the best restaurant in the U.S., located in the heart of Napa Valley. Of course, a meal there doesn't cost $50,000. On the other hand, if you decide to dine there with a friend…every Saturday night…for a year…with $350 to spend on wine to go with your 9-course tasting menu…that's pretty much what it would cost.[x] Would this have been a more enjoyable and more valuable way to spend $50,000 than the fluffy electives I took my last semester in b-school? No doubt.

For **$105,000**, forget a Porsche. Instead, go for the all electric Tesla Model S P85.[xi] It has 416 horses, hits 60mph in 4.2 seconds, and a 17" touchscreen console on the dash. It's also the greenest, safest, coolest, American-made car there is. Period. If you decide to pass up on this car now, you can still drop out after your first year of b-school, make this your consolation prize for not having an MBA, and still possibly come out ahead financially.

For **$170,000** you can stop working altogether and go live in Bali for two years instead of getting an MBA.[xii] I would stay at the two-bedroom luxury "Villa Popo" located in Bali, Indonesia. In addition to the panoramic views of Jimbaran Bay, your stay would include a daily breakfast, household staff, a 15m infinity swimming pool, a living room complete with a 9ft. billiard table, and a poolside BBQ grill with attached dining pavilion. Did I mention it comes with a car and driver to take you to the beach? Start packing...

There's a point to these comparisons besides fantasizing about living in Bali for a few years, as enjoyable as that is! I believe that spending any amount of money greater than a month's rent requires some serious thought. The "investment" framing problem I described earlier will have you thinking of why you *should not* get an MBA, especially if you get into a top school. However, given the costs, the real question is why you *should* get an MBA…the exact same question you would ask yourself before doing anything truly crazy, like moving to Bali or spending every weekend at the French Laundry.

Spending $200,000 for an MBA is truly crazy,

unless you can prove to yourself that it's worth it.

Experience

MBA table stakes are the most important thing to consider before you take the MBA gamble. However, besides the money you put on the table, think about the intangible costs as well. The first cost is that you'll miss two years of work experience and industry knowledge by quitting your job to become a student. There are several dimensions to this problem.

You can get tricked into getting an MBA because you feel like your career hasn't progressed enough *yet*. You get impatient for growth. But, remember that you may be close to the point in your career where your rate of professional growth begins to accelerate. For example, when I left to get an MBA, I was in my late 20's and was just starting to be given large projects and significant responsibilities. My potential to accomplish something was much greater at 28 than at 22 by virtue of my increased skills and industry knowledge. I was also starting to see more new career opportunities.

For example, my "backup" to the MBA was a new position that would have been a big promotion over my existing job. Those two years working would probably have added more to my resume than the previous five combined. After my MBA, all I added to my resume was one line that said "MBA at The Wharton School". That line looked pretty good, but everything below it hadn't changed in two years! It's a mistake to use your previous rate of career growth as a reason to get an MBA. It's more important to figure out whether you're poised for future growth and how this compares to the job opportunities you may have in b-school.

It's also important to think about the rate of change in your industry and whether or not you plan to stay in it. If you plan to switch out, of course this isn't a concern. If you plan to stay in and things move slowly, then you're probably OK as well. On the other hand, if you're staying in a fast changing industry like Technology, be careful. Two years might really be much longer. You can read all the blogs and newspapers you want between classes, but your business connections and industry knowledge will get rusty no matter what.

Finally, it's important to think about whether it's more valuable for your Dream Job to be a specialist or a generalist. I know there are "majors" in b-school, but MBA grads are still considered more generalists than specialists. Think about how much more specialized you could have become with two years of additional work under your belt. For example, I have been doing business development throughout my career and have two years of fewer deals to point to because of the MBA. This dynamic might get even worse if you underestimate your rate of future grow, because you'll miss out on exponentially more experience.

In the end, an MBA is really best for people that want to start fresh on nearly every dimension:

get on a career track with a higher rate of growth, get into an industry with a higher rate of change, or start a new functional specialization. The less these conditions apply, the more job experience and industry expertise you might be giving up simply to get an MBA.

Serendipity

I'm a big believer in serendipity and its ability to completely change your life. If you've been lucky enough to meet That Person at That Place at That Time, you know what I mean. Beyond the personal moments, you also have career opportunities that sneak up on you when you least expect them: your colleague that asks you to leave to start a new company; your client that offers you a new position; or hey, your book about the hidden risks of b-school that becomes wildly popular. You get the idea.

Serendipity doesn't come around often. Each unique opportunity is far more meaningful and full of potential than climbing the corporate ladder. The upside in a corporation is usually just a promotion to the next rung of the ladder. The upside in a new venture is equity or a significant promotion. But, in exchange for the upside potential you'll probably have to take a pay cut. For this reason, the MBA tables stakes can be an obstacle to taking big chances.

When low-paying, high potential opportunities arise, you'll have two options with a financed MBA: First, you can play financing games where you pay less now and pay more later. This could be shifting to a graduated payment schedule on your loans, or going on forbearance to stop your loan payments entirely. Of course, the interest clock will be ticking the entire time, and you can only forbear for a limited amount of time. But, it's something.

The other option is to cut back on your living expenses significantly. However, as we've seen, you need to make tens of thousands of dollars a year just to break-even. Cutting that much fat from your personal expenses is usually impossible. If you don't believe me, make a New Year's resolution to cut $20,000 a year from your family budget, without changing where you live, and see how it goes.

Without an MBA, the downside to serendipity is just the opportunity cost of your prior job. With an MBA, you've made a commitment to one thing before having the freedom to pursuing new opportunities: paying off your student loans. An MBA makes it harder to say, "yes" to serendipity.

The cost of saying "no" to serendipity is impossible to quantify, but hopefully it seems as expensive as it sounds.

GOOD BETS

Bankers

Getting an MBA is a career bet. As we've just seen, it's an expensive bet too. I can't tell you whether your Dream Job is a good MBA bet or not. Doing that analysis is your responsibly. But rather than leave you hanging, I can say that *on average* certain careers are good bets, break-even bets, or one of many sucker bets. Like all heuristics, there are exceptions, but wagering $200,000 on being one of them is a bad idea.

For starters, an MBA is probably a good bet if you want to get into Banking. I don't know many bankers, have never been interested in Banking, and don't claim to know much more than I've accidentally read in The Economist before quickly turning to the Technology section. However, becoming an investment banker, wealth manager, or hedge fund analyst obviously require a firm grip of finance and accounting, and these firms are still willing to pay the big bucks for you to get your MBA.

If you work in the airline industry and think you want to work for Goldman Sachs, then an MBA is a good bet. Ditto if you're in consumer banking and want to transition to investment banking. For the non-finance types, an MBA obviously allows you to claim that you know a thing or two about finance. For bankers at less prestigious banks, if you can attend a school with a better brand than your former employer, you can prove via the rank of your b-school that you're smart enough to work for a better brand of bank.

Puzzlingly, there are people that go to b-school from top banks who return to Banking. If you're already moving up the ladder at Goldman Sachs, I don't know what you have to learn at a top b-school that you can't learn on the job. True, you will learn what it feels like to have sunshine regularly touch your face aside from your two-week annual pilgrimage to the Hamptons. But, when it comes to skills or ability validation, I don't know. My guess is that most Goldman people would end up at the same place after two years in their career path versus two years of b-school. Why you would want to give up two years of bonuses just to drink beer every Thursday with a bunch of people you'll never see again is a mystery to me. Maybe Partners and Clients expect the credential for reputational reasons? Maybe the MBA is your vacation before you return to The Firm to grind out another ten years to make Partner? I have no idea.

Even for aspiring Bankers there's a case to be made that your Dream Job could be obtained in faster and less expensive ways. You could get a one-year Master of Finance: It's one less year of tuition, and you only have to take classes related to banking, as opposed to classes like marketing and operations in the MBA core. You could also get a CFA certification. My guess is that in certain fields a CFA would be just as valuable on the job market, but costs much less to acquire. Again, if you can study during nights and weekends while getting paid and advancing in your existing career, it seems like a much smarter, less expensive option.

I'm not pretending to offer advice to anyone wanting to get into Banking. I'm just not aware of anyone who wanted to get into Banking who had huge regrets about their decision to get an MBA. Similarly, when you look at the salary statistics, many Banking career paths from the top schools seem to be lucrative enough to merit the MBA table stakes. For these reasons, an MBA seems like a good bet when it comes to Banking. But please, don't take my word for it. Ask a real banker before you get an MBA.

Consultants

Consulting is the other industry where an MBA seems like a good bet. You probably only have a vague awareness of this industry, let alone ambitions to become a Partner at one of the big firms. Don't worry. I had barely heard of the big three firms (McKinsey, BCG, and Bain) before b-school. That all quickly changed once I started classes. There's no way in hell you can get through an MBA program without hearing all about them. Most of these firms bombard you with brochures and corporate schwag the second you walk in the door. Every single Top-3 b-school student has a BCG umbrella. My guess is an actual umbrella company is a client and is paying all of their consulting fees with nothing but green umbrellas!

What is this industry that almost no one knows about before school, but where everyone wants to work once they get there? In Consulting, you work very long hours analyzing complicated strategic problems for the Fortune 100. You quickly become a master at making beautifully crafted PowerPoint decks to explain the results of your analysis. You work with extremely smart people on extremely challenging problems. And yes, you make a lot of money to pay off those damn student loans. The only real downside is having 80% travel and very long working hours.

It sounds great, but despite the benefits, there are two things you should think about before you decide to target Consulting: First, many students who want to work in Consulting after b-school, already worked in Consulting before b-school. For them, the MBA is a bet they're taking to upgrade from their current job at Accenture or Deloitte to work for McKinsey or BCG. There's no denying that b-school is a great path into Consulting. However, be aware that if you've never done Consulting before, the competition for the top firms is heavy.

The second thing to consider is that you may end up in Consulting even though you didn't necessarily want to become a Consultant before b-school. Yes, you may honestly change your mind about your goals once you start school. But, you may also feel like it's a more financially pragmatic career compared to your original plans. Put another way, if you don't have an interest in Consulting before b-school, there's a danger you may develop an interest in Consulting during b-school for financial reasons.

This is a risk worth avoiding. It would be stupid to paint yourself into a corner where you're financially incentivized to get a job that you didn't want when you first decided to get an MBA. This is most likely to happen when you go to b-school to "explore your career options" and end up convincing yourself to work in Consulting to pay off those giant student loans you didn't think much about before school. Unfortunately, you didn't explore a new career. You just discovered the best way to quickly pay off your loans.

Let me save you some time. The quickest way to

pay off your loans is to not have any in the first place.

BREAK-EVEN BETS

Career Switchers

If you want to *get into* Consulting or Banking, you should be concerned that many students getting an MBA are Career Switchers who are *just leaving* Banking and Consulting to work for the Fortune 100. Career Switchers use the MBA to get out of jobs with 80-100 hour workweeks and excessive travel, and into middle management jobs with 50-70 hour workweeks and less travel.

Switching careers to a different industry is a problem the MBA solves through the summer internship. Employers get to hire you for a few months after your first year of b-school with little risk. You get a foot in the door to prove yourself in a new role. Employers don't care that you may not have any relevant experience before b-school. They're relying on the brand of your b-school to certify that you're smart enough to be able to learn a new job.

If you think I'm saying that Career Switchers are paying two years of time and tuition to effectively get a summer internship, then you're right. That's exactly what I'm saying. You would think there's a better way. Of course, you could quit your job and try to get an internship yourself. The problem is that you need to be risk-seeking enough to quit, knowing you won't be able to fall back on your second year of b-school if things don't work out. Not everyone has this tolerance for career risk.

The Fortune 100 could get more creative and hire highly qualified, non-MBA summer interns. The problem is that top b-schools attract top students to attend their programs. This makes it easy for the Fortune 100 to target their recruiting efforts. Companies are happy to have their intern pool pre-screened for smart, talented people. For this reason, internships that lead to career switches are tough to find outside of b-school.

Until this situation changes, an MBA remains a reasonable way to get out of Banking and Consulting. However, this is only true if your b-school has a better brand than your current employer. If it doesn't, it's probably worth the risk to try and switch careers on your own. There's no sense in diluting the brand value of your resume unnecessarily.

Compared to aspiring Bankers and Consultants, Career Switchers can be the most creative about avoiding the MBA. This is why I think it's a break-even bet. Yes, there are opportunities to switch careers in b-school. But, there are also tons of things you can do to get into a new career without an MBA: You can move to the hub city for your target industry, such as Silicon Valley for Technology companies. You can get a lower ranking job in your target industry and work your way up. You can brand yourself in a new topic with a book or a blog. You can hire a headhunter. You can organize a conference. The options are only limited by your imagination. And, unless you imagine getting two MBAs back-to-back, all of these options cost much less than a two-year MBA.

Free Money

It's possible to get an MBA with "free money". You (or your parents) might be rich or you might win a great scholarship, but these ways are unusual. The most common way to get an MBA for "free" is to get employer sponsorship. You would think your employer paying for you to go to b-school would be a "good bet". If you work for McKinsey or Goldman Sachs, I would say this is true. But, if you work for a lesser-known company, this is a devil's bargain. In exchange for the "free" MBA, you'll have to work for your sponsor for a few years after you graduate. This means you'll completely miss the option value of working somewhere else.

You might argue that two to three years after you graduate, you will still have a great MBA and new opportunities will still be open. I don't think this is true. The recruiting process is heaviest in b-school when plenty of mid-level positions are available. Once you finish your sponsorship, you'll only find one-off positions that appear at companies randomly. The competition is no longer your fellow students; it's employees that already work at these companies. Current employees know the hiring managers and company politics better than you. Of course, your MBA may give you an advantage over other outside candidates, but overall you have a much lower chance of getting your Dream Job after b-school compared to during b-school.

The other reason it's a bad idea to wait for your

Dream Job until after your sponsorship ends is that your "brand" will not be the b-school you attended. It will be your employer's brand. If your employer has a better brand than your b-school, then it's no problem. If it's the opposite, you'll be giving away brand value to get a free MBA.

The only industry I've seen employer sponsorship work well is Consulting. This is because there are many ways to exit Consulting into other industries and positions. Consultants can go to work for their clients, or their client's competitors. They see a lot of companies and develop skills in specific industries. If you enjoy Consulting and can get sponsored, it's probably a good deal. For any other industry, I would tread carefully unless you want to stay with your sponsor for the long term. As always, there's no such thing as "free".

SUCKER BETS

College Grads

Many students use the MBA to make career bets that have a good chance of paying off. Other students make career bets that are the equivalent of putting all of your chips on black and just spinning the roulette wheel. That's pretty much how I approached b-school. It's an approach I'd strongly urge you to avoid for your own financial health. There are better ways to achieve your goals than relying on luck to succeed.

The first sucker bet is to get an MBA after graduating from college instead of getting a job. Business savvy Universities are quickly realizing what a great up-sell an MBA is for college seniors. At Wharton, there were several undergrads attending the full-time program. HBS has their "2 + 2" program, where you apply for your MBA during your senior year of college and have a guaranteed space at HBS after working for two years. Many other b-schools heavily recruit college seniors as well.

Getting an MBA immediately after college is a mistake.

After you graduate from college, you're trying to find the career path that leads to your Dream

Job. The process is fairly simple: You start with a career hypothesis, collect data, test your hypothesis, and repeat the process until you find it. "I enjoy reading the Wall Street Journal, so I think I'd enjoy Banking" is a hypothesis about a career path. To confirm this hypothesis and generate some data, you could take a class in finance or do a summer internship on Wall St. What's the difference? Working in a bank for three months is pretty damn good data about whether or not you'll like Banking. Studying a single business skill that may only be a small portion of the real job is bad data. One experience helps you find your Dream Job. The other just delays the process, or worse, misleads you about the right path forward.

There are two major problems with getting an MBA right after college. The first problem is that you pay to collect data instead of getting paid. Even worse, you're paying to get bad data about the careers you might like. Taking classes in Marketing tells you nothing about whether you'll enjoy segmenting the market for toothpaste at Colgate-Palmolive. It's much better to get paid to test your career hypotheses in real jobs.

The second problem is that you're limiting your career options at the absolute worst time in your life to do so. When you're 21, you probably don't have a family or significant material possessions. You can sleep on a couch while you work on a startup with your friends, or volunteer in Africa for six months. You can't do these things if you have to pay $2,000 per month in student loans.

Instead, by getting an MBA you're essentially committing to work for a big company right after graduation. That's a lot of option value to throw away for a degree you can easily pursue later.

There are three other things you should think about. First, if you're good enough to get into a top b-school, you're good enough to get hired by a top employer...a much more valuable experience. Second, at b-school you'll be significantly younger than most of your classmates who will be 27-29 years old. You'll have to deal with a lot of rolling eyeballs from your older peers when you make a comment in class based on your *zero* years of experience. Finally, you'll have to deal with the realities of hanging out in the MBA party culture surrounded by old folks trying to re-live the glory days. And you'll be the youngest man or (much worse) woman in the room. Sound like fun?

Don't get an MBA after you graduate from college. Get a job.

Learners

There's a fundamental misunderstanding about b-school. The purpose of an MBA is *not* to help you learn business skills. It's to classify your abilities for the Fortune 100 companies that want to hire you because you've been "pre-approved" by the brand of business school you attend. If you're getting an MBA just to learn business skills and don't really have an interest in getting ranked for the Fortune 100 HR departments, then you're making a mistake.

Unlike law or medicine, you don't need an MBA to practice business. Anyone who can make something worth buying, obeys the law, and pays their taxes is automatically allowed to play the game. If you just want to learn about business but don't need the credential, there are better ways to learn than by going back to school.

The best option would be to explore the world of free learning being ushered in by Massive Online Open Courses (MOOCs), offered by companies like Coursera, Udacity, and edX. All of these companies offer courses in highly practical business topics from the top b-schools. In fact, Coursera even offers the "Wharton Foundation Series", which includes many classes that I myself paid thousands of dollars to take. (Food for thought: I'm five years out of school and already a good portion of the MBA core from my massively expensive degree is online. How long until one of the top schools puts the whole MBA online for free?) All of these courses are free except for your time.

Similarly, in the business areas I'm interested in (entrepreneurship and VC), most of the best learning comes from leaders in the space that blog about these topics (Fred Wilson and Paul Graham are two personal favorites). I can't imagine these business areas are much different from the ones that interest you. There's got to be experts in your industry who are sharing their perspectives, shaped in real-time, in today's market, for free.

Finally, working for other people, for free, is a highly underrated vehicle to learn. This doesn't only mean internships. You can volunteer anywhere to help with regards to a business topic that interests you. My favorite: Pick a non-profit of your choice and try and help them solve a business problem they face in a domain that interests you. Learning by doing is far better than watching lectures or reading blogs.

Have I mentioned that all of these things are completely free? The ROI for free is huge.

Part-timers

Part-time and Executive MBAs seem like good ideas. Part-time MBAs don't have any opportunity cost, and employers often pay for Executive MBAs. In both cases the MBA table stakes are definitely lower. The problem with both of these degrees is that they confuse b-school as a place to learn business skills instead of a place to brand your personal capabilities.

Obviously, the business skills you learn in a full-time or part-time degree are exactly the same. For example, the professors at the full-time Wharton MBA program are the same professors who teach the Executive MBA program. However, getting accepted into a full-time MBA program at a top school is extremely difficult. Getting accepted into an Executive MBA program at a top school isn't nearly as difficult.

If you get a Part-time or Executive MBA, no one will think there's anything particularly exceptional about your abilities. This is especially true of the Part-time MBA, which has a branding problem similar to using the word "part-time" applied to anything else. When someone says "part-time", do you think they work at Google for twenty hours every week, or do you think they're probably a cashier, a barista, or a grocery bagger? Unfortunately, most people think the exact same thing when they hear the words "part-time MBA".

Executive MBAs aren't much better. People

assume that employers simply choose who they want to send, and send them, without any type of competitive selection process. Some people get confused about Executive MBAs and think that the brand of the school is all that matters (without the words "MBA" or "Executive MBA" at the end). The school name has nothing to do with it. An Executive MBA from Wharton is *not* perceived to be as prestigious as a full-time MBA from Wharton, even though the Wharton "brand" is equally as strong. It's not about *the name* of the club; it's about how difficult it is to *get into* the club.

If you can't do a full-time MBA, you shouldn't get an MBA at all. The only exception would be if you need it to get promoted and your company is paying for every nickel. If not, you should find better ways to get the business skills you need. Don't pay for an overpriced Executive MBA, even from a top school. And pretty please with a cherry on top, don't pay $200,000 for a Part-time MBA, which has a branding problem worse than the Republican Party, JC Penney, or the Thunderbird School of Management.

Explorers

When I say "Explorers", I'm not talking about the students that spend $15,000 to go "explore" Antarctica (yes, students actually do this). I'm talking about the people that go to business school to "explore their career options". Explorers have no idea what they want to do after school. They just want to do something *different* from whatever they're doing now. These poor bastards are cursed for several reasons.

Explorers get pulled in every direction. During the first year of b-school, firms are recruiting hard for the best summer interns. You can spend all your free time going to employer info sessions, "coffee chats", dinners, and receptions. And that's just for Consulting, let alone Banking, Technology and everything else. All of these events sound really interesting. So…Explorers try and go to all of them!

Because of this problem, Explorers are more likely to make a bunch of career bets that never pay off. For example, if you decide at the last minute that you want to "do Consulting", you'll probably lose. The students that actually wanted to "do Consulting" have been studying the firms and practicing case interviews for months. You, the Explorer, will be scrambling and cramming for interviews. Even worse, you'll be forced to hedge your bad Consulting bet by applying for other jobs in different industries. In other words, you'll still be exploring!

The side effect of being an Explorer is feeling stressed out all the time. It's impossible to go to every coffee chat and info session. Explorers are always left with the nagging feeling that they're not talking to the right companies. They always feel like they're missing something, because, they are! Until cloning technology drastically improves, you have to focus to win the MBA bet.

If you think it sounds painful to be an Explorer in the first year of b-school, imagine how much worse it would be for you during your second year. Now, instead of cruising through the remainder of your studies with a job in your pocket, you still have to decide what you want to do, and then you have to actually get a job. Take the anxiety from the first year and multiply it by ten.

Why you would ever want to pay $200,000 for the privilege of being stressed out and putting yourself at risk to get sub-par internships and sub-par jobs? Probably because no one ever told you it's a stupid idea.

It's a stupid idea.

Don't "explore your career options" in b-school. Explore your career options *before* b-school. Then, you can pursue very concrete goals and make the most of the opportunity. To do this, use your imagination. Talk to people in the careers that interest you. Study subjects related to these careers. Immerse yourself in books, blogs, and magazines about these industries. Read

McKinsey White Papers if you're interested in Consulting. Start studying for your CFA if you're interested in Banking.

If all else fails, hire a career coach. A career coach will help kick your ass to do the work of uncovering what you truly want to do. Most importantly, they'll help you do this for $50-$200 an hour. If it works, you'll either be able to focus like a laser on your Dream Job in b-school, or avoid the time and tuition altogether. If it doesn't work, just remember that it might not have worked at b-school either. But, paying someone a few hundred bucks is nothing compared to the cost of an MBA.

—

There are too many Explorers at b-school. To solve this problem, every b-school should make career coaching a part of the pre-enrollment process, just like financial modeling. This would be easy to do and relatively inexpensive. Students should be required to complete a certain number of career coaching sessions before enrollment. They should also have access to a database of alumni who can help them learn about different career paths. And, just like with financial modeling, Explorers should receive a "satisfaction guarantee" from b-schools. If they can't figure out what their Dream Job is and how an MBA will help them, they should be allowed to defer admission, or drop out altogether.

B-schools should do this for three reasons: First, students will be happier during their time in school and more likely to achieve their career goals. Second, the entire student body would start b-school more focused on achieving their specific career goals. This should make them better job applicants and improve the school's reputation among employers. Finally, hopefully no Explorer would go to b-school to risk their time and money on a losing bet.

Entrepreneurs

Going to b-school to become an entrepreneur is the worst career bet you can make. I know, because I made this bet and lost. I've also seen many other aspiring entrepreneurs lose this bet as well. Here's why you should never get an MBA if you want to be an entrepreneur.

An MBA is a failure of entrepreneurial thinking. Why? Because you think you need an MBA to start a company, so you spend all your time figuring out how to get an MBA, rather than spending all your time figuring out…*how to start a company*. Worse, you probably believe a bunch of arguments about why an MBA is the "best way" to start a company: "It's the best way to access VC." "It's the best way to find a co-founder." "It's the best way to have time to work on your idea."

A real entrepreneur wouldn't be held back by the idea of needing an MBA in order to do any of these things. A real entrepreneur would find faster, cheaper, smarter ways to do them. They would hunt down VCs at conferences, recruit their best friends to be co-founders, and work nights and weekends to make it happen. Avoiding b-school, as it turns out, is very entrepreneurial.

The arguments that an MBA is the "best way" for anything entrepreneurial are also wrong. You may meet VCs, but if you don't have a real company to pitch them, it doesn't matter. If you do have a real company, having an MBA doesn't matter. You may find a co-founder, but you can meet co-founders at Meetups, industry events, or your current employer just as easily. The time you'll have at b-school to work on your startup idea isn't much more than the nights and weekends you already have, thanks to tons of classes.

Of course MBA graduates start companies, but it's not because of what they learned in school. It's because they were already smart, entrepreneurial people when they got there and were somehow able to beat the odds...just like all the entrepreneurs that *didn't* have an MBA.

Everything that can be done with an MBA can be done without one.

If you've already been accepted somewhere prestigious, consider that going to an elite b-school is not considered an elite accomplishment in the startup world (if it ever was). That honor belongs to the elite startup incubators. It's about Y Combinator, not Stanford. It's about TechStars, not HBS. There's a reason why. To get into a startup incubator, you have to prove you've taken the initial steps to form a business. You build a prototype. You make a sale. You build a website. You get users. On the other hand, to get into b-school, you write an essay and take a math test. There's no prototype, no sale, no website, and no users. Going to b-school is not the first step to starting a company. It's the first step to getting something called an MBA.

If you still decide to get an MBA, you will discover that the two major value-adds of b-school don't matter for entrepreneurs. There are no business skills you need to learn that you can't learn, for free, online. Also, there's no point in branding yourself with an elite credential. You're not trying to work for an employer who cares about your credential. You're trying to work for yourself.

Your potential customers don't care if you have an MBA; they only care about your product. Your potential co-founders and employees don't care if you have an MBA; they only care if you're a good person they can trust. Your investors don't care if you have an MBA; they only care about whether you have customers paying you money. If you're a real entrepreneur, *no one cares about your MBA*.

If you want to become a real entrepreneur, neither should you.

—

Dear b-schools: Let's just call a spade a spade. It's intellectually dishonest to try and convince aspiring entrepreneurs to get an MBA. Worse, it's a waste of one of the most valuable natural resources: people with the risk tolerance and ambition to start a company. In my opinion, aspiring entrepreneurs should be treated with the same deference as endangered animals. Everything in our power should be done to ensure that the entrepreneur "species" flourishes. Spending two years taking classes in accounting and finance for $200,000 is not my idea of a flourishing entrepreneurial environment.

The intellectually honest path is to provide free, online learning resources to help aspiring entrepreneurs understand the steps they need to take to start a company. All other entrepreneurship resources at the school should be converted into short-term, startup accelerators to support seed stage companies. There are two possible models that b-schools should learn about and copy: the Founder Institute and Stanford's StartX Program.

The Founder Institute accepts competitive applications from entrepreneurs that are in the very early stages of starting their businesses. In exchange for a small cash and equity payment, entrepreneurs are surrounded by teams of mentors and inspired to iterate on their idea over the course of four months. *Not two years! Four months.* For many technology concepts, four months is all it should take for someone to figure out if they have a viable concept, or something that is not going to work. Compared to this, the two-year MBA is a lifetime.

The Stanford StartX Program is an incubator for startup teams that include members of the Stanford community, such as students, grad students and professors. It supports these teams, without taking equity, by tapping into the

Stanford community for mentorship and resources. It then co-invests with VCs to further support these companies. The financial returns of the venture fund will hopefully cover the costs to the University of providing these resources. By focusing on the entire University community, StartX can tap into the IP of every university department, and leverage the Stanford business school for support.

Every b-school should do both.

B-schools could easily use their resources to create startup incubators *and* startup accelerators. The incubator would be for students or teams with an idea. The accelerator would be the next level for ideas that evolved into potential companies. Stanford could easily do this today. The b-school could accept candidates from around the world for four-month incubator sessions, three times per year. These students could then join StartX if their ideas were good enough, or exit the program.

This incubator / accelerator model is the best way to support aspiring entrepreneurs.

To prove the point, let's compare the incubator / accelerator concept to the MBA in Entrepreneurship (like I have) on offer today from the top b-schools. From the perspective of an entrepreneur, there is no comparison. In the incubator model you are only committed for four months, or for longer if your company successfully transitions from proof of concept to company building. The cost is perhaps a few thousand dollars or a small amount of equity. On the other hand, an MBA requires a two-year commitment that costs $200,000 and doesn't allow you to pursue your business idea on a full-time basis.

There is simply no comparison between the value proposition of an incubator / accelerator versus an MBA for aspiring entrepreneurs. This is why b-schools should completely eliminate the MBA in Entrepreneurship and replace it with an incubator / accelerator program. It's the only intellectually honest path.

If b-schools can't do this, then they shouldn't do anything at all. Period.

Difference Makers

The new Wharton building is called Huntsman Hall, named after billionaire Jon Huntsman. It's a gigantic, red stone and brick monster with a UFO-like dome at the top. You can see it from across the river in downtown Philadelphia. It's rumored to have a top floor luxury lounge for wooing alumni donors, and has two escalators to take students to and from classes. It has a lot of nicknames, but the best one by far is the "Capitalist Death Star".

Right next to Huntsman Hall, in a little two-story brick building with classrooms in the basement and no escalators, is the School of Social Policy and Practice (i.e. Social Work). Yes, students who have dedicated their careers to helping other people are reminded multiple times a day that their devotion to public service comes at a price. But, don't pity Social Work students. Pity the MBA students that want to make a difference in the world.

Social Work students at least go to school with friends who share their honorable ambitions. There's no risk of "selling out" because nearly everyone is working towards the same goals. On the other hand, Social Work students who decide to go to b-school are surrounded by people more interested in working at a hedge fund than saving the world. You can guess what happens. When you crunch the (poor quality) numbers from the handful of schools that provide it, you'll see below that very few students return to the non-profit world after graduation[xiii].

% OF STUDENTS IN NON-PROFIT, BEFORE & AFTER MBA			
	Before	After	% decrease
University of Chicago	11%	2%	-85%
Harvard University	7%	6%	-14%
University of Pennsylvania	12%	1%	-93%
Stanford University	13%	5%	-62%
Other Top-10 Schools	NO DATA		

What's going on here? One option could be that a lot of non-profit professionals start their MBA, then realize how much money they're spending, and change careers out of pure financial necessity. It could also just be that most students with a non-profit background have no intention of going back. That's OK as well. I'm not trying to suggest that there's anything wrong with heading into the business world if you have a non-profit background. You're free to do whatever you want after b-school and I don't blame you for wanting to make more money.

Either way, if you go to b-school interested in social impact work, you're going to be lonely. There will either be very few students that share your ambitions, or a lot that initially do, but end up in Consulting or Banking after graduation. There are better, cheaper ways to learn business skills and accelerate your non-profit career than getting an MBA.

—

B-schools should be extremely discouraged by the huge number of students who leave the social sector to get an MBA, and then never go back. It means that regardless of what they claim, they're not helping students with noble ambitions follow through after graduation. There's a simple alternative: B-schools should work with the non-profit community to create a tailored academic program for non-profit professionals. Then, they should provide it to as many non-profit professionals as possible for free. Finally, they should make all of these resources available as MOOCs, for free, to everyone.

B-schools raise millions of dollars for fancy classrooms, research centers, and endowments. A few more fundraisers could help non-profit professionals remain that way, by helping them to get exactly the skills they need at no cost to them. Hopefully, this program could be taken on a part-time or short-term basis to allow non-profit professional to stay in their existing jobs.

The point of a separate program is to give non-profit professionals a sane way to learn business skills without having to spend $200,000 to get an MBA. Even though some b-schools offer scholarships to non-profit students, spending two years out of the working world seems unnecessary. A tailored program would also avoid the need for students to take classes that aren't relevant to the non-profit world.

Like entrepreneurship, the social impact sector is an area where the b-school rhetoric and the reality are separated by an intellectual chasm. The good news is that the chasm is really easy to bridge, and the bridge wouldn't cost much money to build.

Let's build it.

Venture Capitalists

Working in the VC industry is a dream for many MBA students. What's not to love about the job? You work with startups, learn about cutting edge technologies, and have the potential to make serious amounts of cash. When you look at the Forbes Midas List, seven of the top ten VCs have MBAs, so it seems like a career path that "requires" the MBA to be successful[xiv]. But, I think the numbers are misleading. Getting an MBA to go into VC is still a bad bet.

Associate positions at VC firms are few and far between. No b-school sends more than a tiny percentage of its students into VC in any given year. This raises a key question: If you don't get hired into VC, do your secondary ambitions mesh with an MBA? Are you interested in Consulting or Banking if VC doesn't pan out? If you're not willing to lose your VC bet and be forced into pursuing your second choice career, don't get an MBA.

A bigger mistake is thinking that having an MBA is all that it takes to get into VC. It isn't. You need to have some serious skills in addition to the MBA to be hired as an Associate. Case in point: There are four Wharton classmates I know who went into VC. Two had science PhDs in addition to an MBA, one had serious operational experience at a successful startup, and one had serious operational experience at a Fortune 100 company in a hot investment area.

In other words, students who get Associate positions have top MBAs *at a minimum*. You need to have serious qualifications to go along with the degree. So, are you VC material without the MBA? Do you have significant technical depth, operating experience at a startup, or expertise in a really hot field of investing? If the answer to all of these questions is "no", then an MBA is not going to make any difference to your chances. You're making a bad bet.

Big picture, the two points above may not even matter. The venture capital industry itself is in the process of radically changing. VC is less and less about putting together a term sheet and being clubby with other VCs from top b-schools. VC is becoming more and more about entrepreneurial credibility and technical credentials. Look at the Partners of the Valley's best new VC shop, Andreessen Horowitz. Less than 25% of the Investment Partners have MBAs[xv]. I would argue that in another 10 years, the Midas List will look the same way. Successful entrepreneurs with technical backgrounds will replace the financial investors with MBAs that came before them.

If you want to get into VC, save your MBA money. Find startups that you can help, and help them. Make micro-investments on AngelList. Refer startups to VCs. In other words, just get out there and act like a VC. Maybe one will hire you. Better yet, if you have a lot of technical depth or serious operational experience, use these skills to start a company. If you're good,

VC can be your retirement instead of your career.

MENTAL MISTAKES

Take the Easy Way

There are a lot of mental mistakes you have to avoid in order to get an MBA for the right reasons. Of all of these, the single greatest mistake is to believe that the MBA is the "only way" to obtain your Dream Job. Be careful. You probably feel that way because an MBA is actually just the *easiest way* to obtain your Dream Job. An MBA is easy because it only takes three steps: You take the GMAT and write some essays. You spend two years studying and getting good grades (like you did in college). You interview and (of course) get hired into your Dream Job. It's a very linear, easy to understand process. But "easy" and "only" are two very different things.

For example, I wanted to become an entrepreneur and felt like an MBA was the "only" way to go. Why? Because b-school had all the easy answers to my unanswered questions. "Where would I find an idea?" In class! "Where would I find a co-founder?" My classmates! "Where would I get funding?" The b-school network! Of course, there were many other answers to these questions. In retrospect, many of them would have been better than getting an MBA. But, I didn't take the time to figure out the alternatives.

If you want to avoid the same mistake, you have to brainstorm every other path you can think of to get your Dream Job. Initially, these other paths will seem more difficult than getting an MBA. Don't worry. Pick the two or three that seem the best. Then, research these alternative paths until you can write down the exact steps that you would take to pursue them. Now, it's a fair fight. The MBA seems easy, but so do the alternatives. You won't feel like the MBA is the only way to go. Instead, you can decide whether or not the MBA is the *best* way to get your Dream Job.

What do I mean by best? The best path towards your Dream Job is the one that is the most *direct* and *inexpensive*. Of course, b-school is both *indirect* and *very expensive*. It's much harder to justify an MBA if you start optimizing for directness and cost. That's good because it means that if you do the research and the MBA seems like the best choice, you can be much more confident that you're making the right decision. On the other hand, if you never go through the process of mapping out the alternative career paths, the only thing you can be confident about is that you're taking the easiest path…and probably paying for every…single…step.

Go to Learn

In your first year at b-school, a common expression floating around the halls is that classes are like "drinking from a fire hose". You're supposed to say this as though you were actually managing to drink some water, as opposed to feeling like hell because of all the water running up your nose.

Here's the problem. Every professor has mountains of homework and readings. These are supposed to be accomplished in team-based case studies where two to three hour daily meetings are normal. Once the team projects are finished, you still have to do your homework, spend time with your family, and of course, go drinking with your b-school buddies. Who could possibly "learn" all that material in this environment? Simple. No one. And no one even pretends to.

You learn to "drink from the hose" by picking one or two classes that you like the best and doing most of the readings and homework for these classes only. For the other classes, you just fake it. You don't raise your hand. You read the case five minutes before class. You bullshit your way through an answer if you're called upon. This is really all that most normal students can manage. A few mental athletes study all the time, but no one reads and learns *all* of the material. It's simply not possible.

This means that you're not paying $200,000 for

two years of intensive learning. You're paying $200,000 to learn maybe two to three classes a semester, because you can only absorb a small amount of what you see and hear. Everything you don't learn ends up in a five-foot tall pile of readings and textbooks that you own after graduation. Of course, you'll never want to look at more than 5% of it ever again.

For example, after graduation I was hired as a consultant to build a financial model. This is the bread and butter of a Wharton MBA. You eat, breath, and drink "Net Present Value". But, building this model I still found myself rifling through old notes and textbooks to remember the most basic things like "What were the conditions where IRR was negative?" "Did NPV start discounting in year 0 or year 1?" It was ludicrous. This was a year after graduation! It's now been five years and I haven't done a financial model since.

Of course, I still remember some things that I've actually managed to use since graduation. But, the rest is like so many other academic classes I've taken…a grade on a transcript and a textbook collecting dust on my bookshelf. What a waste.

Drinking from a fire hose doesn't make you that much smarter…it mostly just gets you wet.

Confuse Luck and Talent

If you're thinking about getting an MBA in the U.S., you know the best schools. There's Stanford and HBS at the top, Booth and Wharton in second place, and everyone else behind them. If you get into one of these top programs, you'll probably think that you were uniquely chosen for your business acumen, leadership experience, and track record of academic excellence.

That's total bullshit.

There are hundreds of amazing people that apply to the top schools and don't get accepted. They're equally as talented as you; they just weren't equally as lucky.

B-schools aren't alone. Luck is such a huge component of the application process for elite Colleges that some people have proposed drawing names out of a hat filled with the best students to determine who gets "accepted".[xvi] It's effectively what happens every day, in every elite MBA program. Except, instead of a random drawing, it's the subjective opinions of a couple of 2nd year b-school students, professors, and administrators.

Let's be honest. Getting into b-school is a lottery system for people with good grades, good test scores, good application essays, and good recommendations. There are many, many more of these people than there are classrooms and chairs at the best schools. I call it the "B-school Lottery". It's a much more accurate description of what happens compared to the term "admissions process".

I'm explaining this for one reason: If you apply to b-school before you've confirmed you're making a good career bet, you run the risk of being accepted. At that point, you're going to be feeling pretty good about yourself. If, God help you, you get into HBS or Stanford, you're going to feel like you walk on water. You'll forget about your questionable reasons for going because you'll feel amazing.

This is a dangerous feeling. Of course you "accomplished something" in that you proved yourself to be "good enough" for the top schools. However, you were also just luckier than the other 5,000 people that applied to the same schools as you. Did you personally have something to do with getting accepted? Sure. But, in addition to your skills, someone on the admissions committee had to make a gut call between you and another person with a very similar background. Somehow they chose you. Maybe they traveled to the same countries you did and your essays about your experiences abroad really resonated with them. Maybe they worked for the same bank you did. Somehow, some other (irrelevant) factor pushed you over the edge.

If you're on the fence about whether you should go to b-school, don't apply until you've made a decision to get an MBA based on an analysis of the alternatives. If you apply and get accepted, *you will go*. It will feel good. You will "know" that you are one of the "chosen", and if you're "chosen", how can you refuse? Your friends will congratulate you and tell you how awesome you are to have been accepted to whatever school. It will be very hard to say "no", when it might be better if you did.

Ignore the Numbers

You can ignore the huge cost of b-school for a long time. Building a financial model before going to b-school is much less enjoyable than daydreaming about trading stocks at Goldman Sachs surrounded by buckets of money. But, there's no avoiding it when the tuition is due your first semester. "Holy shit!" you'll tell yourself "Did I really sign up to take on $50,000 in loans, and will I have to do this again every semester?" Yes, you did, and yes, you will.

There's a big problem with ignoring the MBA table stakes before you attend b-school. Once you're forced to do the math, this newfound knowledge gives you a mental excuse to re-examine your original motivations for attending b-school. It's much easier to doubt your dreams when you're surprised with new information, like the bill for your first semester. This problem is even worse because your self-doubt will be occurring at the exact same time as the start of recruiting season (also known as "the first day of school").

The second problem is that you think less about your original goals and how to make them happen. Instead, you think much more about how to solve the problem of paying for your MBA, after the fact. This is how the people I knew who were interested in working at a startup began to develop a plethora of rationalizations for doing a summer internship on Wall Street. It didn't relate in any way to their original career goals, but it definitely helped them feel like they were solving a financial problem they didn't realize they had until they started school.

The most serious mistake is to ignore the numbers before school and then commit to a career path that can't handle the economics of an MBA. This is exactly the path I took, and the path other aspiring entrepreneurs are at risk of taking. For example, I avoided changing my (financially ignorant) professional convictions by shunning any school function that wasn't related to entrepreneurship. That meant never going to a single coffee chat or interviewing for a summer internship or a full-time job. I avoided thinking of the huge MBA table stakes by convincing myself that I would either be running a successful startup, or that I would be guaranteed a job if my startup failed. Of course, neither turned out to be true.

Ultimately, there's just no way to ignore the numbers. You can ignore them before school. You can ignore them during school. But, you can't ignore them after school. Your lenders will make sure of it.

Want A Break

You probably want an MBA to find a new career, but you may also just want to take a break from working. That's OK, because who the hell doesn't want to take a break? The problem is that you may be thinking about getting an MBA just because you want a break, but don't want to have a dreaded "resume gap". I don't know if employers really care (I have several "gaps" on my resume and no one seems to notice), but I can see why it would be awkward to explain that you took six months between jobs to sit on the beach. It might make you seem less serious than another candidate who never took a vacation.

It's true. Getting an MBA is the next best thing to a break: going back to college. We all remember the early morning classes and the homework. But, we also remember having a lot of free time to do interesting things with interesting people. Going to b-school is kind of like going back to college without any of the negative repercussions of taking a break in a less "legitimate" way, like taking a vacation.

The problem with this "resume gap" thinking is that it discourages you from being more creative and adventurous. I understand that sitting on the beach for six months could be a potential interview problem. However, can anyone seriously say that volunteering for six months would have the same stigma? Or trying to start a new company? Or really, anything but actually sitting on the beach?

The other problem is that while b-school is a "break" from the working world, there's not enough free time for a "productive break." Side projects like volunteering or entrepreneurship will have to compete with tons of classes and preparation for job interviews. You do of course get to sit your ass on the beach quite a bit, but you won't have time to fully immerse yourself in your alternative interests. It's not two years of doing whatever you want. It's maybe a day a week of doing whatever you want. That's not much more time than the nights and weekends you already have.

If you want to take a truly "productive break" like volunteering or writing a book, find another way. You can work with your employer to take a leave of absence. If you're going to leave your job, you confirm that your "productive break" won't have a negative impact on your resume when you return. My guess is that it won't, and as long as you plan for adequate runway to get back into the job market, you'll be fine. Better still, you won't have any debt. You'll just have no savings, no job, and…no regrets.

Believe Rationalizing Alumni

When I first started writing, there were no books on the market talking about why you should *not* get an MBA. Now, there's this one, and one other one published a whopping five months ago[xvii]. It's incredible. The MBA degree has existed for over 100 years since HBS offered the first MBA in 1910. But, in all that time, only two people have taken the time to write a book about the flip side of the coin.

I don't think we're crazy. I just think that once you've spent $200,000 on an MBA, it's pretty hard to admit to yourself that it wasn't the best decision to get one. Even if you have regrets about your MBA, it's probably better for your mental health to rationalize all of the reasons why it was worth the money, the time, and the effort. This is a dangerous fact if you're considering getting an MBA because many MBA grads are "rationalizing alumni".

You can spot rationalizing alumni because they tend to make the following unsubstantiated claims: They "never" would have gotten the job they have now…They "never" would have gained those leadership skills…They "never" would have learned finance…They "never" would have figured out that they were destined for a career in such and such industry…without an MBA.

Rationalizing alumni fail to account for the many non-MBA factors that contributed to their success. They also discount the alternative ways they could have gotten to the same level of success without an MBA. Instead, they have a lot of bumper stickers, hats, and sweatshirts plastered with the name of their alma mater. They will make you feel like you'll never be successful if don't have an MBA.

Much less common, but still out there, are credible alumni. Speak with as many alumni from your favorite school as you need to, until you find one. Credible alumni will speak with you frankly about the pros and the cons of b-school. They know exactly how the MBA helped them in their career and exactly how it didn't. They aren't cheerleaders for their school or the degree. If they give you advice, it's to try to help you make the best decision, not to try and sell you on the reasons you should join the MBA club.

Know the difference.

Ignore the Counterfactual

This is my last essay, so I'd like to leave you with a fun thought experiment: Imagine a pair of twins who are equally capable, who went to the same college, had the same GPA, and now work in the same industry after graduation. The first twin decides to get an MBA. The second twin doesn't. Who would do better in their career over the long run? The one who spent two years and $200,000 to get an MBA, or the one that stayed in their job, gained experience, earned a salary for two years, and took advantage of whatever other opportunities came their way?

What do you think?

My hypothesis is that the non-MBA twin would have a career that was just as interesting as the MBA twin. Why? Because both twins are equally smart, talented, and ambitious! Whatever path they decide to take, they'll both have interesting opportunities throughout their careers and achieve their own successes. Either one could do very well for themselves, or really screw it up. I doubt the MBA would be the determining factor between their successes or failures.

I don't believe that an MBA let's you leapfrog a level or two above the "old you" that decides to keep working for two years, for one reason: *You will never know the counterfactual.* You will never know what you would have done without an MBA. Frankly, you don't really know what you'll do with an MBA! The only thing you know is that you are the same, amazing, talented person, wherever you go to school, and however many letters are behind your name.

It's easy to ignore the counterfactual because it's nice to believe that there are a huge number of business opportunities that are only available to people with MBAs. But is this true? There are no doubt opportunities that are *easier* to obtain with an MBA, but *impossible* to obtain without one? I don't believe it. Neither should you.

If you find yourself thinking that your life will be 180 degrees different because you have an MBA, you're forgetting the counterfactual.

You are still you, whether or not you have an MBA.

RETHINK THE MBA

Four Things

Please do four things when you're done with this book.

Define your Dream Job. Is your Dream Job to be an Associate at Goldman Sachs…a Product Manager at Google…an entrepreneur? Hopefully this is an easy question to answer. If it is, you're ready for the next step. If not, remember the fate of the Explorer and don't go to b-school. Instead, focus your time and energy on finding your Dream Job. First, brainstorm the jobs that interest you. Then, use process of elimination, research, and volunteer work to separate the good from the bad. Use Google, use LinkedIn, use Quora, or even talk to actual people (preferably a career coach). Do whatever it takes to get an answer.

Create a Career Map. Think of your Dream Job as a mountain. A Career Map is a description of each possible path up the mountain. For example, to work as a Product Manager at Google you might: get an MBA, apply for a job at Google that promotes up to Product Manager, or take "Intro to Programming" at Udacity. For each path, take it one step further and describe the concrete steps involved to get there. This will make each path seem less difficult, so you aren't biased to pick the easiest one instead of the best one.

Count the Time and the Money. Estimate the time and money you'll need for every path on your Career Map. Don't worry about the dollars and the days. Estimate the costs within a few thousand dollars, and the time within a few months. Once you have this info, you can choose the path that gets you to your Dream Job as *quickly* and *cost-effectively* as possible. Whether that means you'll have an MBA on your wall is irrelevant. Don't buy a $25,000 Swiss watch if a $100 Timex will still tell you the time.

Execute. Don't second-guess your analysis. If an MBA is the best way to get your Dream Job, go for it! If not, don't try to rationalize how it could be a good idea under this or that circumstance. Be honest with yourself, and don't hold on too tight to what you thought would be the "best" path forward. If the facts change, you're allowed to change your mind too. Believe in your work, make a decision, and execute.

If you take these four steps and are more convinced than ever that b-school is for you, that's great! I hope you get into an awesome school, get a scholarship, land your Dream Job, and get a giant signing bonus when you graduate.

If you've realized that an MBA is not for you, congratulations! You've just saved yourself a huge amount of time and money. Better yet, you now have an alternative plan to get your Dream Job. I'd love to hear from you about how it all turns out.

Finally, there may be a few of you that are more confused than ever about what to do next. An MBA doesn't seem like the best decision, but you're not sure what a better alternative looks like. I understand.

Moving forward, I plan to create more resources to help people who are looking for an alternative to b-school: from entrepreneurship ideas, to creative internship possibilities, to interviews with people who achieved their Dream Job without an MBA. The results of this work will be posted in real-time on the website for this book: **www.rethinkthemba.com.** I hope you'll check it out.

Finally, if you have suggestions that would be helpful, funny MBA stories, or serious questions about your career path, I would love to hear from you and help in any way I can. Please get in touch via e-mail: **micah@rethinkthemba.com** or Twitter: **@rethinkmba**.

Thanks for taking the time to rethink the MBA.

Copyright © 2014 Micah Merrick

All Rights Reserved

This book, or any portion of this book, may not be reproduced, or used in any way without my written permission, except for the use of brief quotations in a book review. Thanks!

www.rethinkthemba.com

ENDNOTES

[i] 2012 mba.com Prospective Students Survey Report
[ii] Ibid.
[iii] Author calculations. See the chapter "MBA Living Expenses".
[iv] BusinessWeek 2012 Rankings; www.poetsandquants.com/school-profile/1-insead/
[v] Assume 9 months per year in school, for a total of (800×9×2)+(5,000×2)+(2,000×2) = $28,400.
[vi] Note to the finance geeks: these numbers are the present value of all interest on these loans for the terms shown. I didn't adjust these numbers based on the limited tax deduction for student loan interest, because most people make too much money after b-school to take the deduction. I also assumed the discount rate is equal to the interest rate to avoid playing discounting games that arises when you have a higher discount rate (the standard 10% number) than the interest rate (e.g. 7%).

[vii] Author calculations; www.finaid.org/loans; Assumptions: 6.8% fixed interest; all debt are Stafford Loans.
[viii] Source: Author calculations; www.finaid.org/loans; Assumptions: 6.8% fixed interest; all debt are Stafford Loans.
[ix] http://www.luxurybazaar.com; Perfect Swiss children to pass watch to when you die, not included.

[x] Estimated cost for the prix fixe menu for 2 people, plus $350 wine budget per meal, plus 20% gratuity.

[xi] http://www.teslamotors.com

[xii] www.balivacationrental.com/villas/popo; Estimated cost for a 2 year stay.

[xiii] Author's analysis. NOTE: Why is this data inadequate? No business school shows the stats for a given class (e.g. Class of 2013). Instead, they show the % of non-profits for the current incoming class only, and then the historic % of graduates who went into non-profit after graduation. In other words, you can never compare apples-to-apples. Instead, we have to assume that the class composition stay roughly the same over time. B-schools should

disclose better data to make better decisions on the part of prospectives!

[xiv] Forbes Magazine's Midas List, 2013

[xv] www.a16z.com/team/; Investment Team biographies as of February 2014.

[xvi] Just one example: Swarthmore Professor Barry Schwartz's column in The Atlantic Monthly: http://www.theatlantic.com/magazine/archive/2012/07/lotteries-for-college-admissions/309026/

[xvii] The other book is "The MBA Bubble" by Mariana Zanetti.

www.ingramcontent.com/pod-product-compliance
Lightning Source LLC
Chambersburg PA
CBHW051722170526
45167CB00002B/758